"Ruhl writes in a poised, c   re
irrational and invisible . . .   ne
pressing existential issues; her stoic comic posture is a means of
killing gravity, of taking the heaviness out of her words in order
to better contend with life . . . Her plays are bold. Her nonlinear
form of realism—full of astonishments, surprises and mysteries—is low on exposition and psychology . . . She writes with
space, sound and image as well as words; her goal is to make the
audience live in the moment, to make the known unfamiliar in
order to reanimate it. *Dead Man's Cell Phone* is a mad pilgrimage
of an imagination as it is invaded and atomized by the phone,
which transforms private as well as public space."

—JOHN LAHR, *New Yorker*

"After you're gone, how will you be remembered? In her new
oddball comedy, Ruhl chews on that question in a smartly enter-
taining way. Ruhl's fascination with death never feels morbid,
because satire is her oxygen. She is a keen observer of social cus-
tom, and there is something forever vital in her lyrical and biting
takes on how we behave."   —PETER MARKS, *Washington Post*

"Ruhl's zany probe of the razor-thin line between life and death
offers some enjoyable insights into modern-day ironies. *Dead
Man's Cell Phone* delivers a fresh and humorous look at the times
we live in."   —PAUL HARRIS, *Variety*

"A captivating, dark-edged romantic comedy with an extraordi-
narily creative premise."
—MELISSA ROSE BERNARDO, *Entertainment Weekly*

"Ruhl makes acute observations about how being surrounded by
wireless devices has eroded public-private boundaries and made
our lives ghostly, atomized and impermanent."

—DAVID COTE, *TimeOut New York*

dead man's cell phone

acknowledgments

Many thanks to Rebecca Taichman and to Howard Shalwitz for all of the love you brought to the first incarnation of this play, for putting your full faith in it. To Anne Bogart and to Tim Sanford for finding the play's second legs with such beauty. And to Jessica Thebus and Martha Lavey for understanding that a play needs a third production to finish the thing—and to Jessica for reading the first, second, third . . . twelfth drafts, of this play, and all the others. To the extraordinary actors who helped me crack this play—to Mary-Louise, forever Z; to Polly, the conscience of the play; to Bill for finding Gordon before he had to leave; to T. for memorizing twelve pages in two days; to Kathleen for the divine spark; and to David, Carla, Kelly, the WADS, Sarah, Jennifer, Naomi, Rick and Bruce for being so open to fabulation. Thanks to all the designers, and to Scott for the open mouth and paper houses. This play was written with the support of the Djerassi Foundation, was commissioned by Sonya Sobieski and Tim Sanford at Playwrights Horizons, and had a reading at the Lark and at New Dramatists early on in its life. Thanks to Annie Cheney for her book *Body Brokers*. Thank you to Sarah Curtis,

PRODUCTION HISTORY

The world premiere production of *Dead Man's Cell Phone* was
produced in June 2007 by Woolly Mammoth Theatre Company
(Howard Shalwitz, Artistic Director) in Washington, D.C. The
production was directed by Rebecca Bayla Taichman; the set
design was by Neil Patel, the costume design was by Kate Turner-
Walker, the lighting design was by Colin K. Bills, the sound
design was by Martin Desjardins, the choreography was by
Karma Camp; the properties master was Jennifer Sheetz; the dra-
maturg was Elissa Goetschius and the stage manager was Taryn
Colberg. The cast was as follows:

A WOMAN, JEAN	Polly Noonan
A DEAD MAN, GORDON	Rick Foucheux
GORDON'S MOTHER, MRS. GOTTLIEB	Sarah Marshall
GORDON'S WIDOW, HERMIA	Naomi Jacobson
GORDON'S BROTHER, DWIGHT	Bruce Nelson
THE OTHER WOMAN/THE STRANGER	Jennifer Mendenhall

The New York premiere of *Dead Man's Cell Phone* was produced
in March 2008 by Playwrights Horizons (Tim Sanford, Artistic
Director; Leslie Marcus, Managing Director). The production

was directed by Anne Bogart; the set and costume design were by G. W. Mercier, the lighting design was by Brian H Scott, the soundscape was by Darron L West and the production stage manager was Elizabeth Moreau. The cast was as follows:

A WOMAN, JEAN	Mary-Louise Parker
A DEAD MAN, GORDON	T. Ryder Smith
GORDON'S MOTHER, MRS. GOTTLIEB	Kathleen Chalfant
GORDON'S WIDOW, HERMIA	Kelly Maurer
GORDON'S BROTHER, DWIGHT	David Aaron Baker
THE OTHER WOMAN/THE STRANGER	Carla Harting

Dead Man's Cell Phone was produced in March 2008 by Steppenwolf Theatre Company (Martha Lavey, Artistic Director; David Hawkanson, Executive Director). The production was directed by Jessica Thebus; the set design was by Scott Bradley, the costume design was by Linda Roethke, the lighting design was by James F. Ingalls, the sound design and original music were by Andre Pluess, the choreography was by Ann Boyd, the fight choreography was by Joe Dempsey and the stage manager was Christine D. Freeburg. The cast was as follows:

A WOMAN, JEAN	Polly Noonan
A DEAD MAN, GORDON	Marc Grapey
GORDON'S MOTHER, MRS. GOTTLIEB	Molly Regan/ Marilyn Dodds Frank
GORDON'S WIDOW, HERMIA	Mary Beth Fisher
GORDON'S BROTHER, DWIGHT	Coburn Goss
THE OTHER WOMAN/THE STRANGER	Sarah Charipar
ENSEMBLE	Géraldine Dulex, Ben Whiting

CHARACTERS

1) a woman, Jean
2) a dead man, Gordon
3) Gordon's mother, Mrs. Gottlieb
4) Gordon's widow, Hermia
5) Gordon's brother, Dwight
6) the Other Woman/also plays the stranger. Has an accent.

SET

1) a moveable dining room table and chairs
2) a moveable café table
3) a cell phone
4) light

notes for the director follow the play

A wonderful fact to reflect upon, that every human creature is constituted to be that profound secret and mystery to every other. A solemn consideration, when I enter a great city by night, that every one of those darkly clustered houses encloses its own secret; that every beating heart in the hundreds of thousands of breasts there, is, in some of its imaginings, a secret to the heart nearest it! Something of the awfulness, even of Death itself, is referable to this. No more can I turn the leaves of this dear book that I loved, and vainly hope in time to read it all . . . It was appointed that the book should shut with a spring, for ever and for ever, when I had read but a page . . . My friend is dead, my neighbor is dead, my love, the darling of my soul, is dead . . . In any of the burial-places of this city through which I pass, is there a sleeper more inscrutable than its busy inhabitants are, in their innermost personality, to me, or than I am to them? . . . The messenger on horseback had exactly the same possessions as the King, the first Minister of State, or the richest merchant in London. So with the three passengers shut up in the narrow compass of one lumbering old mail-coach; they were mysteries to one another, as complete as if each had been in his own coach and six, or his own coach and sixty, with the breadth of a county between him and the next.

—CHARLES DICKENS, *A Tale of Two Cities*

. . . you have done a braver thing
Than all the *Worthies* did;
And a braver thence will spring,
Which is, to keepe that hid.

—JOHN DONNE, "The Undertaking"

In Hopper's paintings there is a lot of
waiting going on . . . They are like
characters whose parts have deserted
them and now, trapped in the space of
their waiting, must keep themselves
company.

—MARK STRAND, *Hopper*

PART ONE

scene one

An almost empty café.
A dead man, Gordon,
sits on a chair with his back to us.
He doesn't look all that dead.
He looks—still.
At another table, a woman—Jean—
sits, drinking coffee, and writing a thank-you letter.
She has an insular quality,
as though she doesn't want to take up space.
An empty bowl of soup sits on her table.
She looks over at the man.
She stares back at her coffee.
She sips.

A cell phone rings.
It is coming from the dead man's table.
It rings and rings.

The caller hangs up and calls again.
Jean looks over at him.
She sighs.
The phone keeps ringing.

JEAN

Excuse me—are you going to get that?

> *No answer from the man.*

Would you mind answering your phone?
I'm sorry to bother you.
If you could just—turn your phone—*off?*

> *The cell phone rings again.*
> *Jean gets out of her chair and walks over to the man.*

Are you ill?

> *No answer.*

Are you deaf?

> *No answer.*

Oh, I'm sorry—

> *Jean signs in sign language:*
> *Are you deaf?*

> *No response.*
> *The phone rings again.*

All right.
Excuse me.

She reaches for the cell phone. She answers it.

Hello? No. This is—you don't know me.

(To the dead man) Are you Gordon?

No answer.

(To the phone) I don't know. Can I take a message?
Hold on—I don't have anything to write with.

She sees a pen on the dead man's table.

(To the dead man) Thank you.

(To the phone) Go ahead.

She writes on a napkin.

How late can he call you?

The voice on the phone begins to sob.

I'm sorry. You sound upset. I'm not—

The caller hangs up.

Gordon?

She touches his shoulder.

Oh—

*She holds a spoon under his nose to
see if he's still breathing.*

*The phone rings again.
She answers it.*

Hello? No, he's not. Can I take a message?

A pause as the person on the other end makes a very long offer.

No, he doesn't want one. He already has one.
No, I don't want one.
I already have one.
Thank you, good-bye.

*She hangs up.
She looks around for help.*

Help.

She dials 911.

Hello?
I think that there is a dead man sitting next to me.
I don't know how he died.
I'm at a café.
I don't know.
Hold on.

She exits with the cell phone to look
at the name of the café and the address.
We just see the dead man and an empty stage.
She returns.

It's on the corner of Green and Goethe. *(Pronounced Go-thee)*
Should I stay with him?
There seems to be no one working at this café.
How long?
Thank you.

> *She hangs up.*
> *A pause.*
> *She looks at him.*
> *His cell phone rings again.*

Hello? No, he's not.
I'm—answering his phone.
Does he have your phone number?

> *Pause while the woman on the phone says:*
> *of course he has my phone number. I am his mother.*
> *The enormity of her loss registers for Jean.*

Oh . . . Yes, of course.
He'll—I'll leave him the message.
Have a—hope you have a—good day.
Good-bye.

> *She hangs up.*
> *She breathes, to Gordon:*

It was your mother.

> *She looks at Gordon's face.*
> *It is transfigured, as though he was just looking at something*
> *he found eminently beautiful.*
> *She touches his forehead.*

Do you want me to keep talking until they get here?
Gordon, I'm Jean.
You don't know me.
But you're going to be just fine.
Well, actually—
Don't worry.

Are you still inside there?
How did you die so quietly?
I'll stay with you.
Gordon.
For as long as you need me.
I'll stay with you.
Gordon.

> *She holds his hand.*
> *She keeps hold of it.*
> *The sound of sirens, rain, and church.*

scene two

A church.
A Mass is being sung in Latin.
Jean kneels down, wearing a dark blue raincoat.
Her cell phone rings.
She looks at it.
She hesitates.
She answers it.
She whispers.

JEAN

Hello?
No, he can't come to the phone right now.

> *On the line, inaudible to us,*
> *a woman says, I know he's dead.*

Oh, you do?

I'm sorry.
Then—why?
Okay, I'll meet you.
What will you be wearing?

A pause while the woman says:
I will be wearing a blue raincoat.

Really? That's strange.
I'll be wearing a blue raincoat, too.
I'll see you then. Good-bye.

Mass continues to be sung.
Jean kneels. She prays.
A spotlight on Jean.

Help me, God.
Help me to comfort his loved ones.
Help me to help the memory of Gordon
live on in the minds and hearts of his loved ones.
I only knew him for a short time, God.
But I think that I loved him, in a way.
Dear God. I hope that Gordon is peaceful now.

The music stops.
A woman comes to a podium.
Mrs. Gottlieb begins her eulogy.

MRS. GOTTLIEB

I'm not sure what to say. There is, thank God, a vaulted ceiling here. I am relieved to find that there is stained glass and the sensation of height. Even though I am not a religious woman I am glad there are still churches. Thank God there are still people who build churches for the rest of us so that when someone dies—or gets married—we have a place to— I could not put all of this— *(She thinks the word grief)* —in a low-ceilinged room—no—it requires height.

A cell phone rings in the back of the church. Jean turns to look.

Could someone please turn their fucking cell phone off. There are only one or two sacred places left in the world today. Where there is no ringing. The theater, the church, and the toilet. But some people actually answer their phones in the shitter these days. Some people really do so. How many of you do? Raise your hand if you've answered your cell phone while you were quietly urinating. Yes, I thought so. My God.

Where was I? A reading from Charles Dickens' *Tale of Two Cities*. A wonderful fact to reflect upon, that every human creature is constituted to be that profound secret and mystery to every other . . . No more can I turn the leaves of this dear book . . . that the book should shut . . . for ever . . . when I had read but a page . . . My friend is dead, my neighbor is dead, my love, the darling of my soul—

Jean's cell phone rings. She fumbles for it and shuts it off. Mrs. Gottlieb looks up and sees the audience.

Well.
Look at this great big sea of people wearing dark colors. It used to be you saw someone wearing black and you knew their beloved had died. Now everyone wears black all the time. We are in a state of perpetual mourning. But for what?

Where was I? Gordon.

Well. I've forgotten my point. Let's have a hymn. Father?

> *A hymn.*
> *Preferably "You'll Never Walk Alone."*
> *The singing begins.*
>
> *Jean's cell phone rings.*
> *Jean sneaks out, covering the phone.*

You'll never walk alone. That's right. Because you'll always have a machine in your pants that might ring. Oh, Gordon.

> *Mrs. Gottlieb sings.*

scene three

A café.
Film noir music.
The Other Woman waiting in a blue raincoat.
Jean enters in a blue raincoat.

JEAN

Hello.

OTHER WOMAN

Hello.
Thank you for meeting me.

JEAN

Not at all.

OTHER WOMAN

We like the same clothes.

JEAN

Yes.

OTHER WOMAN

I suppose that's not surprising, given the circumstances.

JEAN

I don't know what you mean.

OTHER WOMAN

You don't need to pretend.

JEAN

I know.

OTHER WOMAN

Gordon has good taste. You're pretty.

JEAN

I'm not—

OTHER WOMAN

Don't be modest. I like it when a woman knows she's beautiful. Women nowadays—they don't know how to walk into a room. A beautiful woman should walk into a room thinking: I am beautiful and I know how to walk in these shoes. There's so little glamour in the world these days. It makes daily life such a bore. Women are responsible for enlivening dull places like train stations. There is hardly any pleasure in waiting for a train anymore. The women just—walk in. Horrible shoes. No confidence. Bad posture.

The Other Woman looks at Jean's posture.
Jean sits up straighter.

A woman should be able to take out her compact and put lipstick on her lips with absolute confidence. No apology.

The Other Woman takes out lipstick and puts it on her lips, slowly.
Jean is riveted.

JEAN
I've always been embarrassed to put lipstick on in public.

OTHER WOMAN
That's crap. Here—you have beautiful lips.

She hands Jean the lipstick.

JEAN
No—that's—

OTHER WOMAN
I don't have a cold.

JEAN
It's not the germs. It's—

OTHER WOMAN
Put it on. Take your time. Enjoy yourself.

Jean puts on some lipstick.

That was disappointing. Oh, well.

JEAN

I'm very sorry about Gordon. You must be—his friend?

OTHER WOMAN

Gordon didn't tell you much, did he?

JEAN

No.

OTHER WOMAN

Gordon could be quiet.

JEAN

Yes. He was quiet.

OTHER WOMAN

He must have respected you. He was quiet with women he respected. Otherwise he had a very loud laugh. Haw, haw, haw! You could hear him a mile away.

She remembers Gordon.

You must wonder why I wanted to meet with you.

JEAN

Yes.

OTHER WOMAN

You were with Gordon the day he died.

JEAN

Yes.

OTHER WOMAN

Gordon and I—we were—well—
You know. *(She thinks the word—lovers)*
And so—I wanted to know . . .
this is going to sound sentimental . . .
I wanted to know his last words.

JEAN

That's not sentimental.

OTHER WOMAN

I hate sentiment.

JEAN

I don't think that's sentimental. Really, I don't.

OTHER WOMAN

So. His last words.

JEAN

Gordon mentioned you before he died. Well, he more than mentioned you. He said: tell her that I love her. And then he turned his face away and died.

OTHER WOMAN

He said that he loved me.

JEAN

Yes.

OTHER WOMAN

I waited for such a long time.
And the words—delivered through another woman.
What a shit.

The Other Woman looks away.
She wipes a tear away.

JEAN

It's not like that. Gordon said that he had loved many women in his life, but when he met you, everything changed. He said that other women seemed like clocks compared to you—other women just—measured time—broke the day up—but that you—you stopped time. He said you—stopped time—just by walking into a room.

OTHER WOMAN

He said that?

JEAN

Yes.

OTHER WOMAN

Oh, Gordon.

The phone rings.
Jean hesitates to answer it.

Aren't you going to get that?

JEAN

Yes.

She answers the phone.

Hello?

On the other end: who is this?

My name is Jean.
Yes, of course.
How do I get there?

A pause while the mother gives directions.

(To the Other Woman, whispering) Sorry.

The Other Woman shrugs her shoulders.

All right, I'll see you then.
Good-bye.

Jean hangs up.

OTHER WOMAN

Who was it?

JEAN

His mother.

OTHER WOMAN

Oh, God.
Mrs. Gottlieb?
Let me touch up your lipstick before you go.

She does.
Jean puckers.
Music.

scene four

Jean and Gordon's mother, Mrs. Gottlieb, at Mrs. Gottlieb's house.
The house smells of dry cracked curtains that were once rich velvet.
Mrs. Gottlieb wears fur, indoors.

MRS. GOTTLIEB

I don't know why I didn't see you at the funeral.

JEAN

I was in the back.

MRS. GOTTLIEB

Would you say that you tend to blend in with a crowd?

JEAN

I don't know—

MRS. GOTTLIEB

You might wear brighter clothing. Or a little mascara.

JEAN

It was a funeral, so I wore black.

MRS. GOTTLIEB

Fine, fine. That's beside the point.
Gordon left his telephone to you?

JEAN

Yes—he left it to me.

MRS. GOTTLIEB

Why?

JEAN

He wanted me to have it.
Why did you call him on the phone—*after* the funeral?

MRS. GOTTLIEB

I call him every day.
I keep forgetting that he's dead.
I do a little errand, take out my purse, and call Gordon
while I'm stopped in traffic.
It's habit.

JEAN

I'm very sorry. It must be awful to lose a child.

MRS. GOTTLIEB

It is. When someone older than you dies it gets better every day
but when someone younger than you dies it gets worse every day.
Like grieving in reverse.

JEAN

I'm so sorry.

MRS. GOTTLIEB

I see it as my job to mourn him until the day I die.

JEAN

Oh—yes . . .

MRS. GOTTLIEB

Please, sit down.

Jean sits down.

So.

JEAN

So.

MRS. GOTTLIEB

Does anyone continue to call Gordon?

JEAN

Yes.

MRS. GOTTLIEB

Who?

JEAN

Some business acquaintances who don't know that he's dead.

MRS. GOTTLIEB

And do you tell them he's—? *(She thinks the word dead)*

JEAN

Yes.

MRS. GOTTLIEB

I can't bring myself to tell anyone.

JEAN

I understand.

MRS. GOTTLIEB

It's so painful, you have no idea.

JEAN	MRS. GOTTLIEB
No, I don't.	What it's like to lose a child.

JEAN

No.

MRS. GOTTLIEB

You don't have children?

JEAN

No.

MRS. GOTTLIEB

Why not?

JEAN

I might have them, one day.

MRS. GOTTLIEB

You're getting older. How old are you?

JEAN

Almost forty.

MRS. GOTTLIEB

Married?

JEAN

No.

MRS. GOTTLIEB

How do you expect to have children then?

JEAN

I don't know. I could—

MRS. GOTTLIEB

When you're thirty-nine your eggs are actually forty, you know.

JEAN

I could adopt.

MRS. GOTTLIEB

It's better to have your own. They resemble—it's the little ticks—
the family eyebrow—Gordon's eyebrow—

Mrs. Gottlieb makes a little line in the air,
indicating his eyebrow shape.
She tries not to cry.

JEAN

I'm sorry.

MRS. GOTTLIEB

Gordon—and I—had a falling out—you know—after that, he never returned my phone calls—

JEAN

He called you the day he died.

MRS. GOTTLIEB

What? How do you know?

JEAN

Your number was on the out-going calls.

MRS. GOTTLIEB

It was?

JEAN

Yes. It said: Mom.

MRS. GOTTLIEB

Let me see.

JEAN

I deleted it by mistake.

MRS. GOTTLIEB

Gordon called me.

JEAN

Yes.

MRS. GOTTLIEB

He wanted to speak with me.

JEAN

Yes.

MRS. GOTTLIEB

How did you know Gordon, anyway?

JEAN

We worked together.

MRS. GOTTLIEB

Really.

JEAN

Yes.

MRS. GOTTLIEB

No wonder you don't have children.

JEAN

What do you mean?

MRS. GOTTLIEB

Gordon's line of work was—toxic.

JEAN

It could be.

MRS. GOTTLIEB

Did you do the out-going or the in-coming business?

JEAN

In-coming.

MRS. GOTTLIEB

Oh—I see.

Why don't you stay for dinner. Gordon's brother will be here.
And Gordon's wife—you know—his widow.

JEAN

Oh, I wouldn't want to intrude. You must need family time now.

MRS. GOTTLIEB

You knew my son. I insist that you stay.

JEAN

If it would help.

MRS. GOTTLIEB

Yes, I think it would. You're very comforting, I don't know why.
You're like a very small casserole—
has anyone ever told you that?

JEAN

No.

MRS. GOTTLIEB

Are you religious?

JEAN

A little.

MRS. GOTTLIEB

I see. We're not religious. Our name means God-loving in German
but we're not German anymore. Hermia chose a Catholic Mass
for Gordon because she likes to kneel and get up. I did not raise

31

my children with any religion. Perhaps I should have. Certain brands of guilt can be inculcated in a secular way but other brands of guilt can only be obtained with reference to the metaphysical. Gordon did not experience enough guilt. Dinner will be served at seven. Do you eat meat?

                          JEAN

Um—kind of.

                      MRS. GOTTLIEB

Good. We'll be having large quantities of meat. I'm a little anemic, you know. I eat a large steak every day and it just goes right through me.

                          JEAN

Oh, I'm sorry.

                      MRS. GOTTLIEB

So—seven o'clock.

                          JEAN

Seven o'clock. Great. I'm just going to run out for a moment—I have an errand—

                      MRS. GOTTLIEB

Very good, Jean. We'll see you at seven.

Gordon's brother, Dwight.
Gordon's widow, Hermia.
Gordon's mother.
And Jean.
Everyone wears black, except for the mother,
who is in a bright red getup.
A flurry of activity getting to the table.
Everyone sits in the wrong spot.

MRS. GOTTLIEB
Place cards, there are place cards!

Everyone moves, checking place cards,
saying things like:
Oh, oh, sorry, excuse me.

Jean stares at Dwight.
He looks so much like Gordon.
But Jean doesn't want to remind anyone of Gordon's death,
so she doesn't comment on the resemblance.
A silence.

HERMIA

Gordon used to sit—there.

She points at Jean.

DWIGHT

That's right, he did.

JEAN

Oh, I'll move—

MRS. GOTTLIEB

No, no, time to move on, no time like the present.

They all look at Jean for a long moment.
Jean hiccups.

JEAN

Excuse me, I'm sorry. I have the hiccups.

Jean stands up and hiccups.

MRS. GOTTLIEB

There's water through there, dear.

JEAN

Thanks.

Jean exits and hiccups.

HERMIA

What a strange duck.

MRS. GOTTLIEB

Yes, but she knew Gordon. Try to be welcoming, Hermia.

DWIGHT

How'd she know Gordon?

MRS. GOTTLIEB

Work.

Mrs. Gottlieb nods knowingly.
Everyone murmurs knowingly
and says things like:
Really? You don't say. Well . . . Mmm. Hmm . . .

DWIGHT

Out-going?

MRS. GOTTLIEB

In-coming.
Or so she says.

They murmur knowingly.
Jean enters.
A silence.
She sits down.
She hiccups.

JEAN

Oh! Excuse me. My hiccups are so loud.

MRS. GOTTLIEB

Yes, they are, aren't they? Remarkably loud hiccups for such a small woman.

DWIGHT

Mother. Come with me, Jean. I'll show you my secret. It's drinking a glass of bourbon upside down.

JEAN

Okay. *(Hiccup)* Thank you.

Dwight pulls Jean's chair out for her.
Jean and Dwight exit to the kitchen.

HERMIA

Dwight likes her.

MRS. GOTTLIEB

I thought he might.

A silence.

HERMIA

Are you sad?

MRS. GOTTLIEB

Yes, are you?

HERMIA

Yes. So sad that it's—awful. Now I know why they call it awful sad.

MRS. GOTTLIEB

I'm glad we can share this, Hermia. We loved him most of all.

HERMIA

I hope that—the two of us—can continue to—mourn together—Mrs. Gottlieb. I feel so all alone sometimes.

MRS. GOTTLIEB

Call me Harriet.

HERMIA

Harriet.

MRS. GOTTLIEB

I never could get used to Gordon having a wife but now that he's dead you're going to be a very great comfort to me, Hermia.

It is one of the first nice things Mrs. Gottlieb has ever said to her.
Jean and Dwight enter.
Jean is laughing.

DWIGHT

That's better.

JEAN

Dwight got rid of my hiccups!

MRS. GOTTLIEB

You're amazing, Dwight. You have so many hidden talents. Always have. Remember when Dwight was little and he could grow stiff as a board and his friends pretended he was a plank or a dead insect and they would carry him around the living room at my lunch parties and how we all would laugh! Oh. I guess there's no one here to remember that.

A silence.

Well. Let's eat. Rib-eye steak. Do you like rib-eye, Jean? Nothing better in the world, I tell you. Ribbons of flesh, ribbons of fat, all in one bite. Dwight, why don't you carve.

Dwight takes up the carving knife.
He's never carved before. It was Gordon's job.

JEAN

Um—

MRS. GOTTLIEB

A hiccup?

JEAN

No, I'm—

DWIGHT

She's talking, mother.

MRS. GOTTLIEB

Oh!

38

JEAN

I brought some presents for all of you. From Gordon.

DWIGHT

You did?

JEAN

Yes. In his last moments. He wanted to give each of you something. From the café. Before he died. He was thinking of all of you.

Dwight puts down the carving knife.
Jean gets out a little bag of presents.

This salt is for you, Hermia. Because he said you were the salt of the earth.

Hermia takes the salt shaker.
She is moved.

HERMIA

Thank you.

JEAN

And this is for you, Dwight.

Jean gives Dwight a cup.

Because Gordon said you were like—a cup. Because you can hold things. Beautiful things. And they don't—pour out.

Dwight is moved.
He takes the cup.

39

DWIGHT

Gordon said that?

JEAN

Yes.

DWIGHT

Wow.

JEAN

And this is for you, Harriet.

She gives Gordon's mother a spoon.

Because of your cooking.

There is a silence.
Everyone is still.

MRS. GOTTLIEB

What did he mean by that?

JEAN

I—when he was little—and grew up—eating—your food—

MRS. GOTTLIEB

No—

JEAN

It was only a nice—he meant it nicely.

MRS. GOTTLIEB

HE COULD NOT HAVE MEANT THAT NICELY!

Mrs. Gottlieb slams down her chair and exits.
Dwight goes after her.

DWIGHT

Excuse me.

Dwight exits.

JEAN

What did I—?

HERMIA

We never talk about her cooking.

JEAN

I'm so sorry.

HERMIA

Don't worry. She's just—you know.

Hermia plays with her salt.

I love the salt.

Hermia is sad.

Did he use any of it? On his food?

JEAN

Yes, he sprinkled it on his potatoes before he died.

HERMIA

Oh . . . how beautiful . . . His last flavor. Oh.

JEAN

I'm glad you like it.

HERMIA

Yes, I do.

You know, I always thought if Gordon died I'd never want to see my in-laws ever again, and I'd be happy and relieved to never lay eyes on them again, but now that Gordon's dead they sort of remind me of him, and it sort of comforts me. You know?

Mrs. Gottlieb and Dwight enter.

MRS. GOTTLIEB

(To Jean) I'm going to have to ask you to leave.

DWIGHT

We haven't even cut the meat, mother. Jean hasn't eaten—

MRS. GOTTLIEB

All right, Dwight. You seem to know what's best for the household. Why don't you take over now that Gordon's dead. I know that's what you've always wanted. *(With a nasty look at Dwight)*

I'm going to lie down. Upstairs. Hermia—come with me. You can put a cold compress on my head. Dwight—be sure she *eats* something. I'm afraid if she doesn't eat she'll disappear into the *ether.* Poof.

Mrs. Gottlieb and Hermia exit.

DWIGHT

Can I cut you some meat?

JEAN

I'm sort of a vegetarian.

DWIGHT

Oh—I'm so sorry. Why didn't you say so?

JEAN

I didn't want to impose. I think people should be polite when someone cooks a meal for them. Even semi-vegetarians. I mean a foolish consistency is a hobgoblin of little minds. Isn't it?

DWIGHT

I've always thought so.

They look around at the table.

Well—it looks like there's only meat.

JEAN

That's okay.

DWIGHT

Let me look in the kitchen. Hold on.

Dwight exits.
Jean sits alone.
She looks small and tired.
An Edward Hopper painting, for five seconds.
Dwight enters with some caramel popcorn.

How about some caramel popcorn?

JEAN

Okay.

DWIGHT

I'm sorry about my mother.
She can be a little—

JEAN

She must be in a state of shock.

DWIGHT

I guess. She's always got—a little shock—to her.

JEAN

I'm sure she's a nice person, deep down.

DWIGHT

You think so?

JEAN

I think people are usually nice, deep down, when they're put in
the right circumstance. She just must be in the wrong circumstance. A lot. Or something.

DWIGHT

Yeah.

They eat some more caramel popcorn.

You know why my mother named me Dwight?

JEAN

Nope.

DWIGHT

After the president you might think.

JEAN

Oh. Right. Dwight!

DWIGHT

But it's not. It's because my mother felt sorry for the name. She *felt sorry for the name Dwight.* She thought it was ignored, pushed aside. So she named me it. Can you imagine how that would affect a child?

JEAN

Did you feel pushed aside?

DWIGHT

Gordon was the mover and shaker. I always sat back a little.

JEAN

What exactly did Gordon do?

DWIGHT

You don't know?

JEAN

I—

DWIGHT

Even the people at in-coming didn't know?

JEAN

Really? I *love* stationery. Do you do the monograms? And the embossed invitations?

DWIGHT

We do.

JEAN

I love those! When you touch the invitations, it feels so nice. Creamy, and thick, and you can close your eyes and *feel* the words. I think heaven must be like an embossed invitation.

DWIGHT

Yes. Creamy, and flat and deep. Like skin. Or—heaven—you were saying about heaven.

JEAN

I've never sent out an embossed invitation. But I'd like to. One day.

> *Dwight is proud and happy.*
> *Jean is embarrassed for revealing too much.*
> *They both put their hands in the caramel popcorn at*
> *the same time and realize there's none left.*

DWIGHT

Well, we're out of caramel popcorn.
Are you still hungry?

JEAN

A little.

DWIGHT

Let's go out and get us something to eat. Some vegetables.

JEAN

I'd like that.

DWIGHT

You like broccoli? Or zucchini?

JEAN

Sure.

DWIGHT

Which one.

JEAN

Both.

DWIGHT

Great. We'll get some at the grocery store. Then maybe you could come see the stationery store. It's closed now, but I have the key.

JEAN

Okay.

DWIGHT

Mother! We're going out! MRS. GOTTLIEB!
She's ignoring me. She'll be fine.

*A strange unidentifiable sound from far away,
like a door creaking, or a small animal in pain.*

49

JEAN

What's that?

DWIGHT

It's mother crying.

JEAN

It doesn't sound like crying.

DWIGHT

She does it different. Let's go.

scene six

At the stationery store.
The supply closet.
The light is dim.
Jean and Dwight are touching embossed invitations,
closing their eyes.

JEAN

Feel this one. Like a leaf.

Dwight feels it.

This one. Branches. Tablecloths. Wool.

She passes it to Dwight.

This one is my favorite one, though. I'd like to live in a little house
made of this one.

She passes it to Dwight.

DWIGHT

A house made of paper.

Dwight tries to build a little house out of the paper.

JEAN

Yeah.
And this one! Braided hair.

Dwight touches it.

DWIGHT

Can I braid your hair?

JEAN

What?
Okay.

Dwight stands behind Jean and fumbles with her hair.

DWIGHT

Am I pulling too hard?

JEAN

No, that's fine. It feels nice.

You know what's funny? I never had a cell phone. I didn't want
to always *be there*, you know. Like if your phone is on you're supposed to be there. Sometimes I like to disappear. But it's like—
when everyone has their cell phone on, no one is there. It's like

we're all disappearing the more we're there. Last week there was
this woman in line at the pharmacy and she was like, "Shit, Shit!"
on her cell phone and she kept saying, "Shit, fuck, you're shitting
me, you're fucking shitting me, no fucking way, bitch, if you're
shitting me I'll fucking kill you," you know, that kind of thing,
and there were all these old people in line and it was like she didn't
care if she told her whole life, the worst part of her life, in front of
the people in line. It was like—people who are in line at pharma-
cies must be strangers. By definition. And I thought that was sad.

But when Gordon's phone rang and rang, after he died, I thought
his phone was beautiful, like it was the only thing keeping him
alive, like as long as people called him he would be alive. That
sounds—a little—I know—but all those molecules, in the air, trying to talk to Gordon—and Gordon—he's in the air too—so
maybe they all would meet up there, whizzing around—those
bits of air—and voices.

DWIGHT

I wonder how long it will take before no one calls him again and
then he will be truly gone.

JEAN

I wonder too. I'll leave his phone on as long as I live. I'll keep
recharging it. Just in case someone calls. Maybe an old childhood
friend. You never know.

DWIGHT

Did you love my brother?

JEAN

I didn't know him well enough to love him.

DWIGHT

It kind of seems like you do.

JEAN

Were the two of you very close?

DWIGHT

We had our moments. Gordon wasn't always—easy.

JEAN

Tell me a story about him.

DWIGHT

One time Gordon made up a character named Mr. Big X and he said: I'll take you to meet Mr. Big X! I was really excited to meet Mr. Big X. But in order to meet him, Gordon wrapped me up in a blanket and pushed me down the stairs.

JEAN

You have any nice stories about Gordon?

DWIGHT

Yeah. They're just harder to remember, you know. No imprint. Like—one time we had dinner and—Gordon was nice to me— and—what kind of story is that . . .

JEAN

You crying?

DWIGHT

I'm okay.

JEAN

How's that braid coming?

DWIGHT

It's pretty good. I've never done a braid before.

Jean reaches up and feels the braid.

JEAN

It's good. Only you did two parts, not three.

DWIGHT

Huh?

JEAN

Usually a braid has three parts. Two parts is more like a twist. But that's fine. I bet it's pretty from the back.

DWIGHT

It does look pretty.
Here—let me show you—

He tries to show her the twist.
Their faces are close to each other,
in the dark, in the back of the stationery store.
Jean and Dwight kiss.
Gordon's cell phone rings.

Don't answer that.

JEAN

It could be—

DWIGHT

Don't get it. It'll take a message, okay?

JEAN

But I can't get Gordon's messages—I don't have his password! I'll never know who called—

DWIGHT

Their number—on the in-coming calls—will be saved. Okay?

JEAN

Okay.

> *The phone rings.*
> *They kiss.*
> *Embossed stationery moves through the air slowly,*
> *like a snow parade.*
> *Lanterns made of embossed paper,*
> *houses made of embossed paper,*
> *light falling on paper,*
> *falling on Jean and Dwight,*
> *who are also falling.*
>
> *Gordon walks on stage.*
> *He opens his mouth, as if to speak to the audience.*
> *Blackout.*
>
> *Intermission.*

PART TWO

scene one

the last day of gordon's life

GORDON
(To the audience) I woke up that morning—the day I died—thinking I'd like a lobster bisque.

I showered. I had breakfast. Hermia has it timed so she finishes her cereal just as I begin mine. Something proud and untouchable about the way she eats her shredded wheat. A rebuke in the rhythm of her chewing, the curve of her back as she finishes her last bite, standing, washing out the bowl. Who cleans the bowl while they're chewing the last bite? She washes the bowl like this. Getting rid of all the unchewed bits. No respect for the discarded.

I ran to the subway in the rain. I didn't say good-bye. I didn't have an umbrella. I thought about going back for an umbrella, maybe giving Hermia an old-fashioned kiss on the cheek that would soften her face, but I remembered the curve of her implacable back and I forged ahead in the rain, umbrella-less.

You know when people are so crushed together in the rain, in the city, so many people, that no one person needs an umbrella, because one umbrella covers three bodies? And everyone's yelling into their cell phones, and I'm thinking, where have all the phone booths gone? The phone booths are all dead. People are yammering into their phones and I hear fragments of lost love and hepatitis and I'm thinking, is there no privacy? *Is there no dignity?*

I get onto the subway. A tomb for people's eyes. I believe that when people are in transit their souls are not in their bodies. It takes a couple minutes to catch up. Walking—horseback—that is the speed at which the soul can stay in the body during travel. So airports and subway stations are very similar to hell. People are vulnerable—disembodied—they're looking around for their souls while they get a shoe shine. That's when you bomb them. In transit. But I didn't know that then. I was on the subway buried in some advertisement for a dermatology office, thinking about the sale of a cornea. The way I'm talking now—this is hindsight. My mind went: dermatology—cornea—rain—umbrella—Hermia's a bitch—lobster bisque.

I wouldn't really say that I sell organs for a living. I connect people—see: *(Almost sung, as though Iran rhymed with bad)* A man in Iran needs money real bad but he doesn't need his own kidney. A woman in Sydney needs a new kidney but she doesn't need her own cash.

I put these two together. You're a sick person, you want to deal with red tape? You want to be put on hold—listen to bad music on the phone for seven years while you wait for your organs to dry out—is that love? No. Is that compassion? No. I make people feel good about their new organs. I call it: compassionate obfuscation. There are parts enough to make everyone whole; it's just that the right parts are not yet in the right bodies. We need the right man to—redistribute. One umbrella covers three bodies.

Truth for its own sake—I've never understood the concept. Morality can be measured by results: how good do you make people feel? You make them feel good? Then you're a good man. You make people live longer? Great. Is it my job to stop executions in China? I don't have that power. What I *can* do, however, is make sure that these miserable fucks who die for no good reason *have* a reason—I make sure their organs go to someone who needs them.

There was this surgeon I knew who did organ extractions in China—a highly trained surgeon—he couldn't stand it after a while—political prisoners, not even dead yet, made him sick. Now he's a sushi chef in New Jersey. I showed up one day at his counter. I ate his hamachi—excellent. (I don't dip my sashimi in soy sauce. Sushi is for adults. You want to really taste your sushi, taste it. Don't drown it in soy sauce, that's for children.) I enjoyed my food in silence. I thanked him in Chinese. He looked a little startled. People assume he's Japanese. I said to him in Mandarin: you don't want people to know about your old line of work, neither do I. Left it at that. Ate my sushi. You can tell with tuna whether they slice it from the belly or from the tail end. He always gave me the belly. It's the good part.

But that day—the day I died—I didn't want to eat something that reminded me of body parts. I woke up in the morning wanting a lobster bisque. So I get off the subway, go to the café, the place

I always go. A familiar guy behind the counter, a giant, with really huge knuckles. I said, I'll have the lobster bisque. He said, sorry we're out, as though it was a casual, everyday thing to be out of lobster bisque on the day I was going to die, as though I could come back the following week. As though it were a friendly, careless matter—sorry, we're out.

So I said: did you have any ten minutes ago?
And the giant said, yes.
I said, is anyone at this restaurant currently eating a lobster bisque?
And the giant said, well yes.
Who?
And he pointed to a woman in the corner. A pale-ish woman, sort of nondescript.
So I say, I will purchase her bowl of soup.
What? He says. I take out my wallet, pull out a hundred.
Then I see it—she is tilting the bowl to the side to scrape out the last bite.
I watch it go into her little mouth, slow motion.
Son of a bitch, I say. I'll have lentil.

I'm used to getting what I want. But today is not my day. So I have the lentil.

Lentil soup is never that great. It's only ever serviceable. It doesn't really make your mouth water, does it, lentil soup? Something watery—something brown—and hot carrots. Like death. Serviceable, a little mushy and warm in the wrong places, not as bad as you'd think it's going to be, not as good, either.

Suddenly I feel my heart—compressing—like a terrible bird in my chest. And I think—I'm finally punished. Someone is going to sell my heart to someone in Russia. Then I think—use your cell phone. Call your wife. Tell her to give you a decent burial, organs in tact. But the wife's not supposed to know you sell organs for a living. So just call the wife and say good-bye. But no—she doesn't love you enough to have the right tone of voice on your death bed. The kind of voice you'd like to hear—indescribably tender. A death-bed voice.

Gordon having a heart attack, heaving.

No longer holding it in—the things people hold back from each other—whole lives—most people give in at the last moment—but not Hermia, no—she'll be sealed up—she'll keep a little bit extra for herself—that last nugget of pride—she'll reserve it for her tin-can spine—so she'll have an extra half inch of height. That thing—that wedge, that cold wedge between—I can't call her. No. A disappointment. So call your mistress. Or mother. No—mother would say—what a way to die, Gordon, in a café? No, not mother. Dwight? A man doesn't call his brother on his death-bed—no—he wants a woman's voice—but the heart keeps on heaving itself up—out of my chest—into my mouth—and I'm thinking—that bitch over there ate all the lobster bisque, this is all her fault—and I look over at her, and she looks like an angel—not like a bitch at all—and I think—good—good—I'm glad she had the last bite—I'm glad.

Light on Gordon's face, transfigured.

Then I die.

Gordon dies again.
And Gordon disappears.

scene two

Jean and Dwight in a love haze
in the back of the stationery store.

DWIGHT

I was dreaming about you. And a letterpress. I dreamed you were
the letter Z.

JEAN

Why Z?

DWIGHT

Two lines—us—connected by a diagonal. Z.

JEAN

Oh, Dwight.

DWIGHT

If we are ever parted, and can't recognize each other, because of death, or some other calamity—just say the letter Z—to me—it will be our password.

JEAN

Z.

DWIGHT

Let's never be parted. I don't need more than twelve hours to know you, Jean. Do you?
Tell me you don't. We exchanged little bits of our souls—I have a little of yours and you have a little of mine—like a torn jacket— you gave me one of your buttons.
I—I love you Jean.

The phone rings.

Don't get that.

JEAN

It'll just take a second.
(To the phone) Hello?
Are you sitting down?
This might come as a very great
shock to you.   DWIGHT
But Gordon has passed away.   Jean? Who's on the phone?

JEAN

I'm sorry, who is this?
(To Dwight) a business colleague.
(To the phone) The funeral was yesterday.

Yes, it was a very nice service.
It was Catholic so it wasn't very personal—
I'm sorry—are you Catholic?
Oh, good—I mean—

DWIGHT

(Whispering) Jean—come here . . .

The voice on the phone offers Jean his condolences.

JEAN

(To Dwight) I'm on the phone!
(To the phone) Yes, in-coming. Thank you,
but if you want to offer condolences,
the best thing would probably be to
write to Hermia and Harriet Gottlieb.
Their address is 111 Shank Avenue.

DWIGHT

(No longer whispering) Jean!

JEAN

(To Dwight) I'm on the phone!
(To the phone) I don't know anything about a living will—no—
I'm sorry. I have to go.
I hope you have a pleasant day
in spite of the bad news.
Good-bye.

She hangs up.

DWIGHT

Who was that?

JEAN

A business colleague.

DWIGHT

I don't think you want to get mixed up in that.

JEAN

Oh, Dwight, I'll be all right.

DWIGHT

I forbid you to talk to Gordon's colleagues.

JEAN

You *forbid* me?

DWIGHT

Get rid of the phone. Give it up. It's bad luck.

JEAN

It brought me to you, didn't it?

DWIGHT

It's not good for you. Life is for the living. Me. You. Living. Life, life, life!

The phone rings.

If you answer that phone, Jean, if you answer that phone—

JEAN

What?

DWIGHT

I will!—
it will make me sad.

JEAN

I have to answer it, Dwight.
Sometimes it seems like you didn't even love your own brother.

She answers it. Dwight crumples.

(To the phone) Hello?
Jean speaking.
(To Dwight) It's Hermia.
She needs a ride home.

scene three

Hermia and Jean
drinking cosmopolitans.

HERMIA

Give me another. Don't worry, I can drive home after all, Jean.

JEAN

You think so?

HERMIA

If I drive with my face. Haw haw haw! Oh, God, I sound like Gordon.

JEAN

You must have a lot on your mind. Do you want to talk?

HERMIA

Yes, in fact, I would. Lately I've been thinking of the last time I had sex with Gordon. Over the last ten years, when Gordon and I would have sex, I would pretend that I was someone else. I've heard that a lot of women, in order to come, pretend that their lover is someone else. Like a robber or Zorba the Greek or a rapist or something like that. Do you ever do that?

JEAN

No.

HERMIA

But you know what Jean? I pretended that *I* was someone else, and that Gordon was Gordon, but he was cheating on me with me—*I* was the other woman. And it would turn me on to know that Gordon's wife—me—was in the next room, that I—the mistress—had to be quiet, so that I—the wife—wouldn't hear me. You and I both know that Gordon had affairs.

JEAN

Well—

HERMIA

So the last time I had sex with Gordon I wish I could say that I wasn't pretending. That he was really in me, and I was really in him. But I was pretending to be a co-worker of Gordon's. He brought her to dinner once. That night, she was wearing a thong under a white pantsuit. (I never wear a thong. It's like having a tampon in your asshole, don't you think?) Anyway, that last time, I imagined myself in this white pantsuit, and his hands under my thong, ripping it off. I pictured what Gordon was seeing—and I picture me, looking back at Gordon. And there is more and more desire, like two mirrors, facing each other—it's amazing what the mind can do.

After I met you, I was convinced that you and Gordon were having an affair. So after dinner, I was—you know—and I pretended to be you—and it worked. Isn't that a riot?

JEAN

That's—um—

HERMIA

I wouldn't normally tell you that but I've had a lot to drink at this point.

JEAN

You should know that I didn't have a sexual relationship with your husband.

HERMIA

Then why do you have his fucking phone?

JEAN

I was the last one with him.

HERMIA

And why was that, Jean?

JEAN

A coincidence.

HERMIA

Gordon didn't have coincidences. He had accidents. There's a difference.

The phone rings.

Give that to me.

She rips the phone out of Jean's hands.

Oops—missed the call!
Is his picture of the Pope still on it? From a business trip to Rome.
Those mobs at the Vatican, waving their cell phones, stealing an
image of the Pope's dead face, and Gordon among them. I can still
hear him laughing, I have the Pope in my pocket. There it is.
Dead Pope. Oh, I feel sick.

The phone rings again.

I'm going to bury it. Like the Egyptians.

JEAN

No.

Jean gestures for the phone. The phone keeps ringing.

HERMIA

Yes, in the ground, with Gordon. There was this Belgian man
very recently in the news and the undertakers forgot to remove
the cell phone from the coffin and it *rang* during the funeral! Just
went on ringing! And the family is suing for negligence Jean—
for *negligesh*—you have to *bury* it, see—to *bury* it—very deep so
you cannot hear the sound.

The phone stops ringing.

Are you ever in a very quiet room all alone and you feel as though
you can hear a cell phone ringing and you look everywhere and

you cannot see one but there are so many ringing in the world that you must hear some dim echo. Nothing is really silent anymore— and after a death— an almost silence—you have to bury it bury it very deep.

JEAN

I'm sorry, Hermia, but I can't let you do that. Gordon wanted me to have his phone.

Hermia hands Jean the phone.

HERMIA

Do you know what it's like marrying the wrong man, Jean? And now—now—even if he *was* the wrong man, still, he was *the* man—and I should have spent my life trying to love him instead of wishing he were someone else.

What did Charles Dickens say? That we drive alone in our separate carriages never to truly know each other and then the book shuts and then we die? Something like that?

JEAN

I don't know what Charles Dickens said.

HERMIA

What good are you, Jean. You don't even know your ass from your Dickens. Oh, God! Two separate carriages and then you die!

Hermia weeps.

JEAN

Hermia. There's something you should know. Gordon wrote you a letter before he died. There were different drafts, on napkins,

all crumpled up. The waiter must have thrown them out, after
the ambulance came, but I read one of the drafts.

HERMIA

What did it say?

JEAN

I forget exactly. But I can paraphrase. It said, Dear Hermia. I know
we haven't always connected, every second of the day. Husbands
and wives seldom do. The joy between husband and wife is elu-
sive, but it is strong. It endures countless moments of silent
betrayal, navigates complicated labyrinths of emotional retreats.
I know that sometimes you were somewhere else when we made
love. I was, too. But in those moments of climax, when the dark-
ness descended, and our fantasies dissolved into the air under the
quickening heat of our desire—then, *then,* we were in that room
together. And that is all that matters. Love, Gordon.

HERMIA

Gordon knew that?

JEAN

I guess he did.

HERMIA

Well, how about that.

> *Years of her marriage come back to her with a new light shining
> on them.*

You've given me a great gift, Jean.

JEAN

I'm glad.

HERMIA

What can I give you?

JEAN

Nothing.

HERMIA

You gave me back ten years of my marriage. You see, after I learned that Gordon's "business trips to Rome" equaled him, trafficking organs, I couldn't bring myself to—. You know— people never write into *Cosmo* about how sexual revulsion can be caused by moral revulsion—they just tell you to change positions.

JEAN

Organs?

HERMIA

Oh, yes, Gordon and his organs—
that's funny Gordon rhymes with organs, how is it I've never noticed that—
Gordon, organ/organ, Gordon, same letters too!
O, R, G—there's no D—
and God in the middle—oh! I feel sick.

JEAN

Gordon—sold organs?

HERMIA

I thought you were in in-coming.

JEAN

I was.

HERMIA

And you didn't know what was in the packages?

JEAN

No—I guess I didn't.

HERMIA

That's funny! Well, I'm sorry to ruin your illusions about
Gordon. I was never supposed to know—I told my friends he was
in waste management. I remember one sad case. Gordon convinced a Brazilian man to give his kidney to a woman in Israel.
Gordon paid him five thousand dollars cash. Gordon probably
made one hundred thousand dollars in the transaction. He
bought me a yellow diamond. (I think they look like something
you'd find in a candy machine, but they're very rare.) So the man
returned to Brazil, kidney-less. And then his money was stolen
from him at the airport in Rio. Can you imagine? He wrote these
sad letters to our home. He would draw pictures of his lost kidney. It looked like a broken heart.

JEAN

Oh!

The phone rings.
Jean and Hermia look at each other.
Jean chooses to answer it.

Hello—

She is cut off.
She listens for a while.
Film noir music.
She hangs up.

They said they have a kidney from Brazil. Go to South Africa. To the airport. I'll be wearing a red raincoat. And hung up.

I have to go to South Africa.

                    HERMIA
What?

                    JEAN
I'll make up for Gordon's mistakes.

                    HERMIA
Too late, Jean. The kidneys, the corneas, the skin—they're the rings on my fingers and the fixtures in our bathrooms. What's done is done.

                    JEAN
Someone is *waiting* for a kidney, Hermia!
Tell Dwight I'll call him from Johannesburg.

                    HERMIA
What?
Jean! Do you own a gun?

    But Jean is out the door.

scene four

At the airport in Johannesburg.

Jean waits.

A stranger enters (the Other Woman who is disguised completely and androgynously with a different accent from the one she had before— she now has an Eastern European accent, whereas before she had a vague, worldly and wholly unidentifiable accent of a beautiful woman who travels constantly between the city capitals of Europe and South America).

Film noir music.

The stranger wears a red raincoat and sunglasses.

The stranger takes her cell phone out and dials a number.

Jean's cell phone rings.

She answers it.

JEAN

Hello.

STRANGER

Hello. I am right behind you.

Jean looks back at her.

Don't look at me.

Jean turns back.
They remain on their phones though they are in close proximity.

Place the money on the lost luggage counter. Then hang up, and place your phone on the lost luggage, as though it is afterthought. Then check your watch, look distracted, look up at departure screen, and get back on a plane to your own country.

JEAN

Actually, we're in a bit of a pickle. In our country we can only give our organs away for love. I mean I'm not saying our country is great or anything because at the moment—well, you know—but in terms of organ laws—it has to be love. It's a strange law, right, because how can you measure love? I'm not sure you *can* measure love.

In any case, if you're willing to give away your kidney for love, then we're still in business. If not—

I am willing to give my kidney away instead of yours.

STRANGER

What?

77

JEAN

That's right. It was so good of you to offer. I'm sorry I have no money to give you. I did make something for you though, just a token, it's a lamp, in the shape of a kidney, it says, I was willing to give you away so that someone else shall live—so that when you turn it on—

STRANGER

Hang up the phone. I'm coming over.

They hang up their phones.
The stranger approaches.

There are numbers stored on that phone. I need them.

JEAN

You can't have it.

STRANGER

I advise you to hand it over quietly.

JEAN

No, I won't. I won't!

STRANGER

Hand over the phone or I will kill you.

JEAN

That's absurd. You can't have it.

The stranger pulls out a gun.

78

STRANGER

You know nothing of Gordon's work, do you? It's big business.
You're in over your head.

JEAN

No—I'm afraid you're in over *your* head.

Jean kicks the gun out of the stranger's hand.
Jean kicks the stranger on a special part of her leg so that she
crumples to the ground.

(Surprised at her own daring) Whoa!

A struggle for the gun.
The stranger grabs it.
She points it at Jean.

STRANGER

I didn't want to have to do this, Jean, but you are forcing my
hand—

The stranger hits Jean on the head with the gun.
Jean falls to the ground.
The lamp falls and breaks.
A flash of light.

scene five

Jean and Gordon sitting at a café.
As if we are at the top of the play.
You might imagine taking gestures from the very first scene
and repeating them in the following
as though Jean and Gordon are doomed to repeat
their first encounter over and over again for eternity.
Jean, sitting in front of a bowl of empty soup.
A silence.

JEAN

Do they have lobster bisque in heaven?

Jean looks up at Gordon.

GORDON

We're not in heaven. We're in a hell reserved for people who sell organs on the black market and the people who loved them.

JEAN

Gordon?

GORDON

That's right. When you die, you go straight to the person you most loved, right back to the very moment, the very place, you decided you loved them. There's a spiritual pipeline, you might say. In life we are often separated from what we love best—errors of timing, of geography—but there are no errors in the afterlife. You loved me most, Jean, so you came to me.

JEAN

What if the person you loved most didn't love you most?

GORDON

Don't try to work it out. It's too complex. Mathematical hoopla. If they need three of *Jean the beloved* why they make you into three Jeans. For the very few it's a neat transaction—totally reciprocal. *A* loves *B*, *B* loves *A*. However: some mothers loved their children best, those children loved their father best, and the father loved the family dog. Some end up with gardens. The very best parents loved all their children equally but that is rare, rare.

JEAN

How about people who loved God best?

GORDON

Don't know. Never met 'em. They go to a different laundromat.

JEAN

Laundromat?

GORDON

See you only have one costume here. Whatever you died in. So you go to the laundromat once a week. Only you have to wash your clothes naked. It's weird—hundreds of naked people washing their socks.

JEAN

Who did you love best?

GORDON

I loved myself best of all. There's a special holding pen for us. Waiting to see if someone else will join us. Like you joined me, Jean. You're my good luck.

JEAN

But I'm not dead.
You're lying.
You lie all the live long day.

GORDON

No, *you* lie all the live long day.
All those nice lies you made up for me?
Now why did you do that, Jean?

JEAN

I saw you die. I saw your face. I wanted for you to be good.

GORDON

Aw, Jean.

JEAN

Oh, Gordon.

GORDON

You and I—we're alike. We both told lies to help other people. You decided to help a dead man because only a dead person can be one hundred percent good. When you're alive, the goodness rubs off you if you so much as leave the house. Life is essentially a very large brillo pad.

But I digress. The point is, Jean, we're two peas in the proverbial pod. In-coming calls, out-going organs, we're all just floating receptacles—waiting to be filled—with meaning—which you and I provide. It's a talent, and I admire you.

JEAN

No—we're not alike. You made people into *parts*, into things. Don't you feel bad about that?

GORDON

I feel done with it—that's all. Money and organs and trade—up here—it's just road kill of the mind. I'm done with organs. Didn't even donate mine. They're all intact. I never signed that little thingy on my driver's license. Felt like a suicide note to sign it . . . and now . . .

JEAN

You don't need them.

GORDON

No.

JEAN

Take them out.

GORDON

What?

JEAN

Take them out. Put them on a cloud and lower them into South
America for all the sad people who sold their own.

GORDON

Would that make you feel better, Jean? Would it?

JEAN

Yes, I think it would.

GORDON

All right, Jean.

> *Gordon puts his hand under his shirt.*
> *He tries to remove his kidney.*
> *He tries a couple of ways.*
> *He turns his back to the audience.*

I can't get it out, Jean. I can't get it out.
Oh, I've almost got it Jean!
I can feel it coming out!
Help me get it out! It won't come out!
The skin is so tough! Uuuuugh!

> *He turns back around.*
> *His organs are still in place.*

Couldn't do it.

JEAN

Oh God, how did I end up in your pipeline? Why am I not here
with Dwight? In a stationery store. I loved Dwight, didn't I?
I don't even know you.

GORDON

You love me because I'm charismatic. I'm more charismatic than
Dwight. Even dead, apparently. I spent about two seconds feeling
guilty about that when I was a child, then I just went on being me.
Sorry, Jean. You have to be very careful who you fall in love with,
and where. A nondescript café for all time? Couldn't you have
chosen better wall hangings? Or better weather? An overcast day,
for all time?

JEAN

I liked it when you couldn't talk.
Could you—pretend to be dead again? Just for a moment?

GORDON

Whatever turns you on, Jean.

> *He pretends to be dead.*
> *She looks at him.*
> *She holds his hand.*
> *She tries to feel her old love for him.*
> *She looks in his eyes.*

JEAN

What were you looking at before you died?

GORDON

You.

JEAN

Me.

GORDON

Yes, you were eating the last bite of my soup. But I wanted you to have it. That's why my eyes looked so nice—I was giving you my last bite. They say love goes right through the eyes—bam. I saw you before I died; you didn't see me. You saw me after I died; I couldn't see you. We had star-crossed eyes. Now we can gaze and gaze for all time . . .

They kiss a strange kiss.

We don't really kiss with our mouths up here. Just letting you get the hang of it.

JEAN

What do you kiss with?

GORDON

Our hair.

JEAN

Oh, God!
I am dead, aren't I?

GORDON

Yes.

JEAN

I suddenly feel very lonely.

86

GORDON

You can still listen to the others, you know. Invisible conversation.
They're still in the air—listen:

A recording of Jean:
Should I stay with him?
There seems to be no one working at this café.

JEAN

(To Gordon) You can hear cell phones here?

GORDON

Oh, yes. The only communication device God didn't invent was
gossip, and that's the most advanced technology to date. It's what
they call the music of the spheres—listen—

A cell phone ballet.
Beautiful music.
People moving through the rain
with umbrellas, talking into their cell phones,
fragments of lost conversations float up.
Jean listens.

Then, Mrs. Gottlieb enters.

MRS. GOTTLIEB

Of course he has my phone number, he's my son, I'm his mother.
Who is this? Gordon?

Mrs. Gottlieb exits.

JEAN

I heard her voice. On your phone. I thought—what can you tell a
mother—about her dead son. I said: have a good day. And then
I kept on lying to her, to make up for it.

GORDON

Ah, mother.
She was never so comforting in life as she was in death. If mother
did not approve, then mother did not appear to love. Funny.
I never knew whether or not my own mother loved me.

JEAN

Oh, she loved you.
Your mother is beside herself with grief.

GORDON

No lies, Jean.

JEAN

No lies. Not that you deserve it.
Your mother said: I see it as my job to mourn him until the day
I die.

GORDON

She did?

Jean nods.

How about that. My mother loved me after all.

Gordon's face, aglow from loving his mother best.

JEAN

Gordon—your face is different.

GORDON

How?

JEAN

You look well-loved.

Gordon?

GORDON

Mother?

Gordon disappears.
He is sucked into a cosmic pipeline
attached to his mother's hell.

JEAN

Gordon?
Gordon!

A silence.
Jean, alone in the afterlife,
an Edward Hopper painting.

It's so quiet.
I'll just call Dwight.

Turn on. Turn on.
Stupid, stupid phone.

It won't go on.

I'll just pretend it's working.
Hello, Dwight, if you get this message,
I am alone on my own planet
and I might be here for all time because I didn't tell you I love you
in the closet in the dark of the stationery store
because I got scared and then the phone rang
and when something rings you have to answer it.
Don't you?

STUPID STUPID PHONE!

> *She throws the phone down.*
> *She bangs it on the ground until she destroys it.*
> *It is the first time in a long time she has let herself cry.*

Z.
Z!

> *She disappears.*
> *Jean reappears on some lost luggage in the airport.*
> *Dwight appears.*

DWIGHT

Jean!

JEAN

Oh, Dwight! You have no idea what I've been through!

DWIGHT

Jean! I told you! You should never have gone off with those bad
people! I forbidded you.

JEAN

You were right, Dwight! Dwight you were right! Did you get my message? I called you from my planet. It was so cold. And the air, oh it remembers, it all stays, like an Irish whistle they hear us. Did you hear me? Z!

DWIGHT

Oh, Jean!

JEAN

Can we go home? Do I have my kidneys? Does knowing someone help to love them best or does it all happen in one millisecond? I let your brother go. No phone. Oh, Dwight—call me darling.

She collapses in his arms.

DWIGHT

Oh, Jean, oh darling.

scene six

Dwight carries Jean to his mother's home.
Mrs. Gottlieb, holding a glass of bourbon.

DWIGHT

Mother! Jean passed out in Johannesburg.

Dwight tends to her.
Jean looks at Mrs. Gottlieb.

JEAN

Hello? Who are you? Put down your weapon!
Oh, Dwight!

DWIGHT

Here, have some bourbon, upside down.

She does.

MRS. GOTTLIEB

A lot has happened since you've been here, Jean. Hermia has had an offer to return to the stage.

JEAN

The stage?

MRS. GOTTLIEB

The ice follies. Hermia used to be a world-class dramatic skater, but Gordon thought it was undignified for his wife to dance on the ice wearing loud makeup. So she left the follies for him. Let that be a lesson to you, Jean. Never leave off follies for a man. Well, now the follies have her back. She's on tour. Denmark, then San Jose.

Hermia, in the distance, ice dancing.
Dramatic skating music.

And I for one am happy for her. Dwight has been using his letterpress to publish books of subversive political theory and poetry—haven't you, Dwight? He's on all the government watch lists.

JEAN

But I've only been gone a day—

MRS. GOTTLIEB

No no Jean you've been gone months.

JEAN

That's not possible.

MRS. GOTTLIEB

Oh, yes. And Gordon's mistress—Carlotta—she's taken over his business—yes—she got hold of his old business contacts somehow and away she went.

Carlotta, in the distance, brandishing a phone.

JEAN

It was her!

MRS. GOTTLIEB

He left her nothing, you see, in the will—and she'd been with him twelve years. Gordon should have been more generous. Everyone's moved on. Except for me.

He was my only son. That is to say—he was my first son. The first sometimes feels like the only—you must know that from your own sexual experiences, or are you a virgin Jean?

DWIGHT

Mother! What would make you feel better, Jean?

MRS. GOTTLIEB

A cold compress, a quiche?

JEAN

I think I'd like a steak actually.

MRS. GOTTLIEB

A steak? I thought you didn't eat meat.

JEAN

I'm starving.

MRS. GOTTLIEB
Carmen! PUT A STEAK ON THE FIRE!
Rare?

JEAN
Yes!

MRS. GOTTLIEB
RARE!
You know, I've tried to call Gordon but his voice is no longer on the out-going message. I call his old number, and no voice. And somehow—now—I feel he's truly dead.

JEAN
I have something to tell you, Mrs. Gottlieb.

MRS. GOTTLIEB
Well then don't stand on ceremony, dear.

JEAN
Gordon's gone up the pipeline to spend eternity on your planet since it seems you loved him most.

MRS. GOTTLIEB
What?

JEAN
It's hard to explain. You won't understand until you die.

MRS. GOTTLIEB
You've seen Gordon?

JEAN

Oh, yes.

MRS. GOTTLIEB

That's where you've been?

JEAN

Yes.

MRS. GOTTLIEB

And he's waiting for me there? In heaven?

JEAN

It's a kind of heaven, I guess. There are these—laundromats.

DWIGHT

Laundromats?

MRS. GOTTLIEB

Does he have to do his own laundry?

JEAN

Yes he has to do it himself now.

MRS. GOTTLIEB

Is he punished?

JEAN

Not really. Now he's with you. Or—he's waiting for you.

MRS. GOTTLIEB

For me alone?

JEAN

Yes.

MRS. GOTTLIEB

He has no one else to console him?

JEAN

No.

MRS. GOTTLIEB

Gordon! Gordon, I'm coming!

Together we'll play all the games we played when you were little.
Hush, little wormy, on my arm, we'll get a spider to calm you
down! Gordon, wait for your mother! It won't be long now!

JEAN

Wait, don't!

Mrs. Gottlieb walks off with determination.
She might sing a reprise of "You'll Never Walk Alone."
She throws herself into the flames with the steak
and self-immolates, but we don't need to hear or see that.

The fire—the steak on the fire—oh no—the pit—
it's such a large barbeque in the backyard—
Aren't you going to stop her?

DWIGHT

No. They'll be happy together.
She always did love him best.

JEAN

So that's that?

DWIGHT

Good-bye, mother. Kiss my brother for me and be happy.

JEAN

Oh, Dwight.
I want to make sure we get on the same planet when we die.
I don't want to end up with my garden or my dog for all time.
Let's start loving each other right now, Dwight—
not a mediocre love, but the strongest love in the world,
absolutely requited.
I want to be selfish with you.
I want to love you because of and not in spite of
your accidental charms.
I want to love you when you burn the toast
and when your shoes are awful
and when you say the wrong thing
so that we know and all the omniscient things of heaven know
too—let's love each other absolutely.

DWIGHT

Then let's do it, Jean. Let's love each other better than the worthies did.

JEAN

Who are the worthies?

DWIGHT

It's from a poem.

JEAN

Did you write it?

DWIGHT

No John Donne did. I'll take you to my letterpress and show you.

JEAN

Now?

DWIGHT

Not right now.
Now we kiss. And the lights go out.

They kiss,
and the lights go out.

The end.

NOTES FOR THE DIRECTOR

On the cell phone ballet . . .

I kept a record of conversations I overheard on cell phones as
I was writing this play to use as found text in the cell phone ballet. The notion was that fragments from the ruin float up and
meet Jean—and that they are almost beautiful. The problem is
that when you record found text with actors' voices, it no longer
feels authentic, because the voice itself is not found. You might
then consider going around and recording people's overheard cell
phone conversations. Or use messages that have already been left
on your phone. If you choose to use my own text to layer over the
music of the spheres, here are the most useful found bits of text
that I've incorporated into different productions:

> I'm disappointed in you—I thought you could stay on—
> there was more than a million dollars involved—I
> talked to Jack—in human resources—

You have to sign the death certificate at the top and at the bottom—that's all—

I love you

Yes, Dr. Stevens, thank you I can come in then for the biopsy—or should we make it later? Eleven?

Do you know how it hurts when you pick up the phone in that tone of voice?

I love you.

Good-bye

You might consider layering these bits into a song, or spoken over a song, having them vaguely sung, or not, having non-actors record them, finding bits of your own found text, or translating some or all of it into Japanese and various other languages. And if all else fails, cut the cell phone ballet and keep the repeated voices of Jean and Mrs. Gottlieb. It rankles me to be this vague, but the cell phone ballet depends so much on the sound designer, director, and all the rest of it. As for choreography, there might be a simple *pas de deux* while people are on their cell phones, or the movement might be as simple as people walking through the rain carrying umbrellas while talking on cell phones. One thing I learned is that if the movement is complex, the music and voices should be simple; if the voices are complex, the movement should be simple. I wish I could tell you there is one definitive way to crack this oyster but it's up to your collective imagination.

As for the Edward Hopper moments . . .

I think they are about finding one simple gesture—Jean looks toward a window—and suspends—and the lights imperceptibly shift. They are about the solitary figure inside the landscape or architecture. They are about being alone inside of or in relation to the modern.

As for the Mandarin . . .

You might want Gordon to speak actual Mandarin instead of English when he says, "I said in Mandarin"; here is one translation of "you don't want people to know about your old line of work, neither do I":

nǐ bù xī wàng bié rén zhī dào nǐ yǐ qián de gōng zuò wǒ yě bù xī wàng

Translation generously provided by Jason Rudd.

As for everything else . . .

There is a great deal of silence and empty space in this play, but the pauses should not be epic.

There might be an extended fight sequence in the airport in Johannesburg as they struggle for the gun.

I call Jean's stories confabulations, I never call them lies . . .

The paper houses that fall on Jean and Dwight at the end of Part One should ideally be made of high quality or handmade paper. Go to a paper store and touch the paper.

Transitions are fluid. Space is fluid. There is not a lot of stuff on the stage.

Enjoy yourself.

SARAH RUHL's plays include *Dead Man's Cell Phone* (Helen Hayes' Charles MacArthur Award for Outstanding New Play or Musical), *The Clean House* (Pulitzer Prize Finalist, 2005; The Susan Smith Blackburn Prize, 2004), *Passion Play* (The Fourth Freedom Forum Playwriting Award from The Kennedy Center, a Helen Hayes Awards nomination for best

ANTHONY CHARUVASTRA

new play), *Eurydice*, *Melancholy Play*, *Orlando*, *Demeter in the City* and *Late: a cowboy song*. Her plays have been produced at Arena Stage, Berkeley Repertory Theatre, the Goodman Theatre, Lincoln Center Theatre, Madison Repertory Theatre, the Piven Theatre, Playwrights Horizons, Second Stage Theatre, South Coast Repertory, Steppenwolf Theatre Company, The Wilma Theater, Woolly Mammoth Theatre Company and Yale Repertory Theatre, among others. Her plays have also been produced in London, Germany, Australia, Canada and Israel, and have been translated into Polish, Russian, Spanish, Norwegian, Korean and German. Originally from Chicago, Ms. Ruhl received her M.F.A. from Brown University where she studied with Paula Vogel. In 2003, she received a Helen Merrill Emerging Playwrights Award and a Whiting Writers' Award. She is the recipient of the MacArthur Fellowship. Ms. Ruhl is a member of 13P and New Dramatists.